Introduction

In all of my years in business, I have never seen our great field leaders so excited about the opportunity we have in front of us. Our leaders are focusing on the right things, building tremendous teams and realizing record-breaking cash flow.

This is the dawn of The Golden Era in HGI. Our greatest leaders are prepared to enter a new era of Discipline and Accountability, which will lead to Ascension and Dominance.

Now is the time to increase our intensity. We must take our game to an even higher level to maximize this tremendous opportunity.

All aspiring legends of the future must focus on these key areas immediately to explode your business and experience quantum growth:

1. The New Supercharged Video Drop System/"The Play"
2. The Eight Speed Filters
3. The HGI Field Building Program
4. 100% Commitment to Quantum Growth

Your future takes a giant leap forward right now by becoming a student of the HGI Leadership Format System. Then, through the relentless repetition and copying our blueprint for success, you possibly can make your dreams come true, as many others have before you, by using our proven, duplicable turnkey system.

The purpose of this book is to highlight the key focal points of the Leadership Format System manual to help you Unlock the Secrets of the System. You still must study the LFS manual in its entirety to fully master the system.

HGI was built for people who want to be somebody. This is your moment. Now is the time for you to seize the day and conquer your future.

Hubert Humphrey

Hubert Humphrey
Founder and CEO
Hegemon Group International

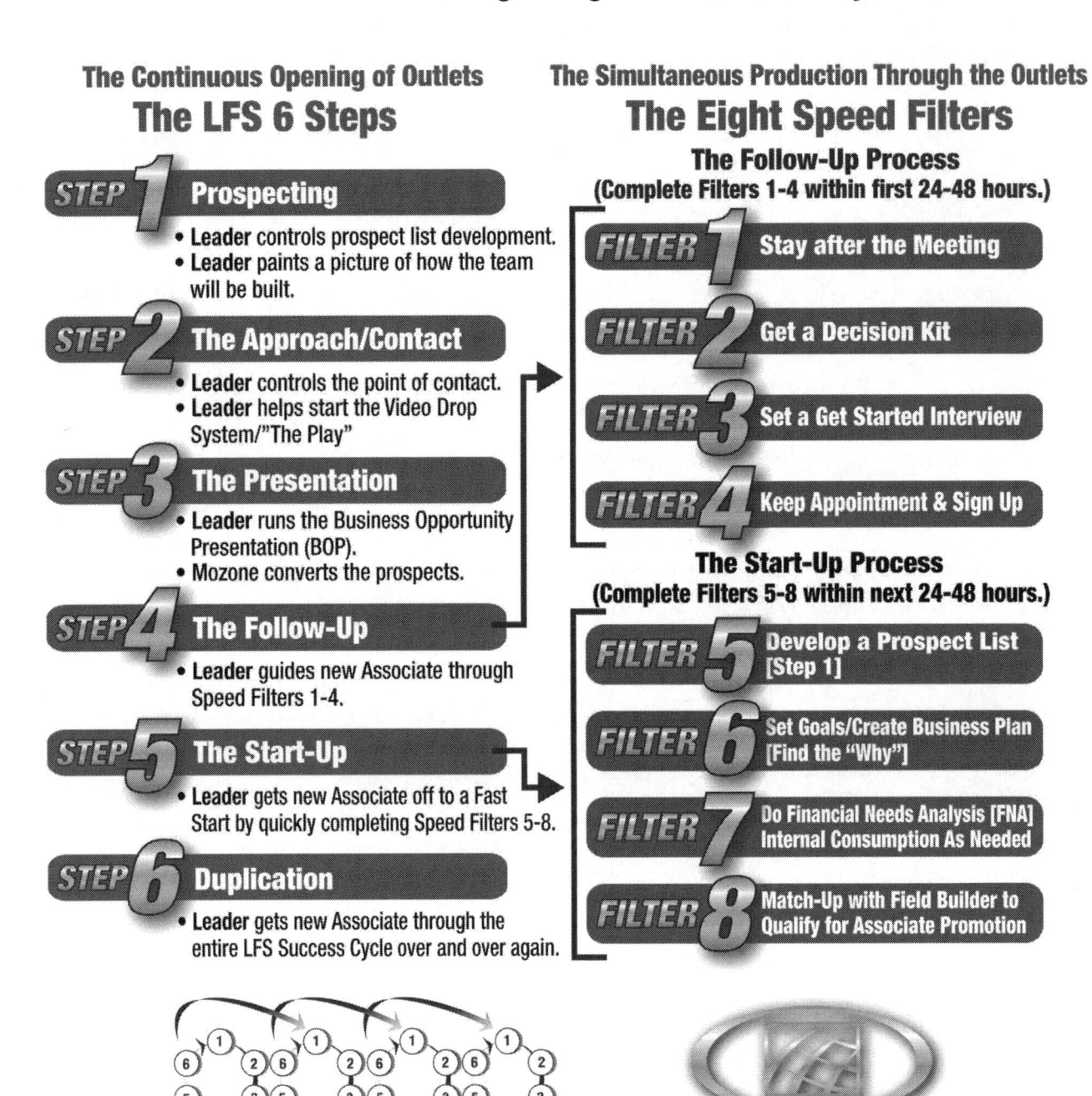

The Leadership Format System

The rapid relentless repetition of these 6 recruiting steps
can lead to the building of a giant distribution system.

The Continuous Opening of Outlets
The LFS 6 Steps

STEP 1 — Prospecting
- **Leader** controls prospect list development.
- **Leader** paints a picture of how the team will be built.

STEP 2 — The Approach/Contact
- **Leader** controls the point of contact.
- **Leader** helps start the Video Drop System/"The Play"

STEP 3 — The Presentation
- **Leader** runs the Business Opportunity Presentation (BOP).
- Mozone converts the prospects.

STEP 4 — The Follow-Up
- **Leader** guides new Associate through Speed Filters 1-4.

STEP 5 — The Start-Up
- **Leader** gets new Associate off to a Fast Start by quickly completing Speed Filters 5-8.

STEP 6 — Duplication
- **Leader** gets new Associate through the entire LFS Success Cycle over and over again.

The Simultaneous Production Through the Outlets
The Eight Speed Filters

The Follow-Up Process
(Complete Filters 1-4 within first 24-48 hours.)

- **FILTER 1** — Stay after the Meeting
- **FILTER 2** — Get a Decision Kit
- **FILTER 3** — Set a Get Started Interview
- **FILTER 4** — Keep Appointment & Sign Up

The Start-Up Process
(Complete Filters 5-8 within next 24-48 hours.)

- **FILTER 5** — Develop a Prospect List [Step 1]
- **FILTER 6** — Set Goals/Create Business Plan [Find the "Why"]
- **FILTER 7** — Do Financial Needs Analysis [FNA] Internal Consumption As Needed
- **FILTER 8** — Match-Up with Field Builder to Qualify for Associate Promotion

For educational and training purposes only.

The Leadership Format System Flow Chart

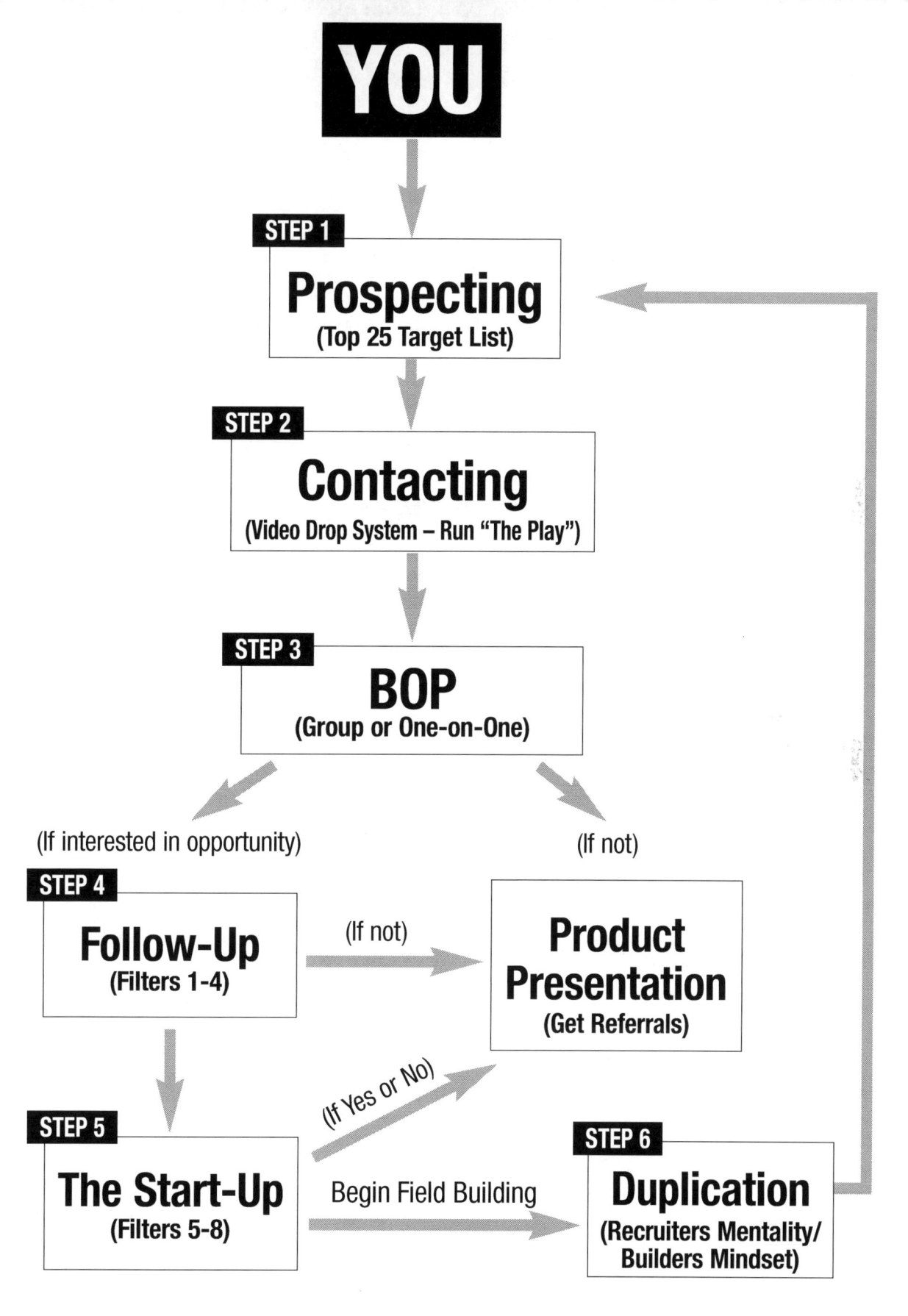

YOU

STEP 1
Prospecting
(Top 25 Target List)

STEP 2
Contacting
(Video Drop System – Run "The Play")

STEP 3
BOP
(Group or One-on-One)

(If interested in opportunity) / (If not)

STEP 4
Follow-Up
(Filters 1-4)

(If not) →

Product Presentation
(Get Referrals)

STEP 5
The Start-Up
(Filters 5-8)

(If Yes or No)

Begin Field Building

STEP 6
Duplication
(Recruiters Mentality/ Builders Mindset)

For educational and training purposes only.

STEP 1: Prospecting

Developing a Target Market

Purpose: To max out and organize your available resources to attract the people necessary to accomplish your goals.

Just as a building contractor cannot construct a building without a large supply of raw materials, a Hegemon Group International empire builder needs a large pool of prospects to plug into the Hegemon Group International System to build a distribution empire.

You can divide prospecting into three areas:

1. Natural Market
- Friends, neighbors, relatives, co-workers, social contacts, business contacts
- Anybody and everybody

2. Friendship Farming
- Turning strangers into friends to create a new natural market.

3. Friendship Borrowing System
- Relationship marketing through our third-party referral system.

CREATE A TARGET MARKET LIST

Making a target market list should be a top priority of any new Associate.

Make the list the start of an exciting business adventure. From this list, you'll build a business and potentially transform the lives of the people on it.

1. Add names, don't eliminate them.

Resist the tendency to eliminate people from your list because you think they're too busy or make too much money. That is a major mistake. Remember, it's not just who you know, but also who they know. Use the Memory Jogger to help you add as many names as possible to your list.

2. Identify the "Top 25" on your list.

Your list should have a minimum of 100 names to start and grow to as many as 300 or even 500. But once you develop your list, you need to quickly identify the "Top 25" and begin contacting them immediately with your leader. The people on your "Top 25" list should have the following general qualifications:

- 30+ years old
- Married
- Dependent children
- Homeowner
- Solid business/career background
- $40,000+ household income
- Dissatisfied

TOP 25 TARGET MARKET LIST

Date: _____
Associate: _____
RMD: _____

	Name	Spouse	F/A[1]	Home Number	Office Number	Profile[2]	Contact Date	Results	BOP	MA[3]	Data	Client
1												
2												
3												
4												
5												
6												
7												
8												
9												
10												
11												
12												
13												
14												
15												
16												
17												
18												
19												
20												
21												
22												
23												
24												
25												

[1] (F) Friend/ (A) Acquaintance
[2] Profile
(1) 30+ Years
(2) Married
(3) Dependent Children
(4) Homeowner
(5) Solid Business/ Career Background
(6) $40,000+ Household Income
(7) Dissatisfied
[3] Membership Agreement Signed and Fees Paid

HGI — HEGEMON GROUP INTERNATIONAL

STEP 1 Prospecting

Memory Jogger

1. Work With
2. Boss
3. Partner
4. Elevator Person
5. Landlord
6. Security Guard
7. Vending Sales
8. Secretary
9. Typing Pool
10. Caterer
11. Customer
12. Parking Attendant
13. Coffee Shop
14. Car Pool
15. Personal Manager
16. Sales People
17. Boss's Lunch
18. Lunch With
19. Competition
20. Repair Person
21. Copier Person
22. Union
23. Complainer
24. Inspector
25. Credit Union
26. Pension Plan
27. Fired-Up Male
28. Fired-Up Female
29. Delivery Person
30. Express Mail
31. U.P.S.
32. Mailman
33. Lost Job
34. Almost Lost Job
35. Will Be Laid Off Next
36. Has Been Laid Off
37. Job Hunting Male
38. Job Hunting Female
39. Hates Job
40. Missed Last Promotion
41. Walking Encyclopedia
42. Most Likable
43. Needs Part-Time Job
44. Engineer
45. New Employee
46. Operator
47. Payroll
48. Contractor
49. Movers/Shakers
50. Guard
51. Preacher
52. Nurse
53. Dentist
54. Doctor
55. Surgeon
56. Chiropractor
57. Therapist
58. Carpenter
59. Auto Mechanic
60. Car Sales
61. Body Repair
62. Gas Station
63. Teacher
64. Substitute Teacher
65. Banker
66. Teller
67. Policeman
68. Highway Patrol
69. Home Builder
70. Painter
71. Roofer
72. Insulator
73. Landscaper
74. Wallpaper Hanger
75. Carpet Layer
76. Hospital Worker
77. Department Store
78. Grocery Store
79. Convenience Store
80. Waitress
81. Waiter
82. Chef
83. Cashier
84. Dishwasher
85. Auto Supply
86. Electrician
87. Hardware Store
88. Truck Driver
89. Pharmacist
90. Funeral Director
91. Flower Shop
92. Health Spa
93. Restaurant Business
94. Dry Cleaner
95. Electronics Store
96. TV Repair
97. Furniture Repair
98. Movie Rental
99. Appliance Person
100. Cable TV
101. Eye Center
102. Tire Store
103. Realtor
104. Office Supplies
105. Copier Salesperson
106. Vacuum Cleaner
107. Phone Installer
108. Pest Control
109. Cosmetic Sales
110. Carpet Cleaners
111. Golf Pro
112. Appliance Repair person
113. Bowl With
114. Hunt With
115. Golf With
116. Fish With
117. Tennis With
118. Ski With
119. Throw Darts With
120. Softball With
121. Baseball With
122. Football With
123. Soccer With
124. Racquetball With
125. Handball With
126. Swim With
127. Fire Chief
128. Fireman
129. Volunteer Firefighter
130. Scout Master
131. Den Leader
132. Barber
133. Beautician
134. Auctioneer
135. Sells Siding
136. Family Pictures
137. Photographer
138. Guidance Counselor
139. Youth Director
140. Sister-In-Law
141. Brother-In-Law
142. Father-In-Law
143. Mother-In-Law
144. Brother
145. Sister
146. Father
147. Mother
148. Cousin
149. Aunt
150. Uncle
151. Grandfather
152. Grandmother
153. Niece
154. Nephew
155. Best Friend
156. Spouse's Best Friend
157. Farmer
158. Army
159. Navy
160. Air Force
161. Marines
162. Baby-Sitter
163. Sister's In-Laws
164. Neighbor On Right
165. Neighbor On Left
166. Across Street
167. Behind
168. Down Street
169. Parent's Right
170. Parent's Left
171. Best Man
172. Maid Of Honor
173. Matron Of Honor
174. Bridesmaids
175. Ushers
176. Fellow Church Members
177. Plumber
178. Jaycees
179. Play Bridge
180. Play Bingo
181. Table Tennis
182. Pool
183. Trivial Pursuit
184. Monopoly
185. Rides With
186. Jogs
187. Runs Track
188. Basketball
189. Plays With Kids
190. Climbs Mountains
191. Hang Glides
192. Karate
193. Your Principal
194. Your Teacher
195. Your Coach
196. Kid's Principal
197. Kid's Teacher
198. Kid's Coach
199. Music Teacher
200. Piano Teacher
201. Hates To Lose
202. Loves To Compete
203. Lamaze Class
204. Kiwanis
205. Lions Club
206. Rotary
207. Good Cook
208. Friend's Parents
209. Lawyer
210. Highway Department
211. Professor
212. Sunday School Teacher
213. Child's Sunday School Teacher
214. Chamber of Commerce
215. Hotel Business
216. Printer
217. Surveyor
218. Radio Announcer
219. Sportscaster
220. Writer
221. Journalist
222. Editor
223. Publisher
224. Tanning Salon
225. Arcade
226. Baker
227. Librarian
228. Accountant
229. Machine Shop
230. Paints Billboards
231. Pilot
232. Stewardess
233. Steward
234. Air Traffic Control
235. Ambulance Driver
236. Travel Agent
237. Antique Dealer
238. Armored Car
239. Telephone Operator
240. Piano Tuner
241. Service Station
242. Sign Painter
243. Who You Camp With
244. Locksmith
245. Upholsterer
246. Veterinarian
247. Notary Public
248. Orthodontist
249. Dance Teacher
250. Loves Seafood
251. Wears Contacts
252. Computer Repair
253. Computer Sales
254. Cabinet Master
255. Bookkeeper
256. Architect
257. Best Fund Raiser
258. Tree Surgeon
259. Railroad Conductor
260. Game Warden
261. Cab Driver
262. Bus Driver
263. Cat Lover
264. Dog Lover
265. Animal Trainer
266. Doll Maker
267. Direct Sales
268. Social Worker
269. Makes Good Fudge
270. Health Food Shop
271. Seamstress
272. Bookworm
273. Likes To Sing
274. Likes To Eat
275. Lawn Maintenance
276. Cellular Phone
277. Rotisserie League
278. Satellite TV
279. Internet
280. Computer Whiz
281. E-Mail List
282. Voice-Mail List
283. On-Line Service
284. Laptop Computers
285. Software
286. Computer Games
287. Desktop Publishers
288. Travel Agent
289. Trainer
290. Works Out With
291. Gym Members
292. Club Members
293. Facebook
294. Twitter
295. MySpace
296. Linked In
297. YouTube
298. Google +
299. Pinterest
300. Live Journal
301. Tagged
302. Instagram
303. Cafemom
304. Ning
305. Meetup
306. My Life
307. My Yearbook
308. Badoo

NOTES:

STEP 2: The Approach/Contact

Controlling the Point of Contact

Purpose: To effectively contact a prospect and set a date to attend the next Business Opportunity Presentation (BOP) at the office, or alternatively, a one-on-one BOP in the next 24-48 hours.

THE APPROACH/CONTACT

There are two proven methods you can use in the approach/contact phase. The key is choosing the most effective method given the circumstances, and the nature of the prospect you're trying to approach.

- **The Video Drop System**

  The most effective way to contact new prospects about the HGI opportunity is the Video Drop System. Utilize the most powerful recruiting tools ever known – with video links at (hgiplay.com) and powerful HGI brochures – to run "The Play" and take HGI's Video Drop System to an entire new level.

- **The Invitation Script**

  Using HGI's time-tested approach, you can effectively contact your natural market while avoiding the "Scenario of Disaster." You must master the art of becoming a mobile inviter.

For educational and training purposes only.

STEP 2: The Approach/Contact

Controlling the Point of Contact

Purpose: To effectively contact a prospect and set a date to attend the next Business Opportunity Presentation (BOP) at the office, or alternatively, a one-on-one BOP in the next 24-48 hours.

Controlling the Point of Contact

Mastering a quality "Invitation Script" is the proven method of avoiding the "Scenario of Disaster." Remember, you must control the point of contact.

"Scenario of Disaster"

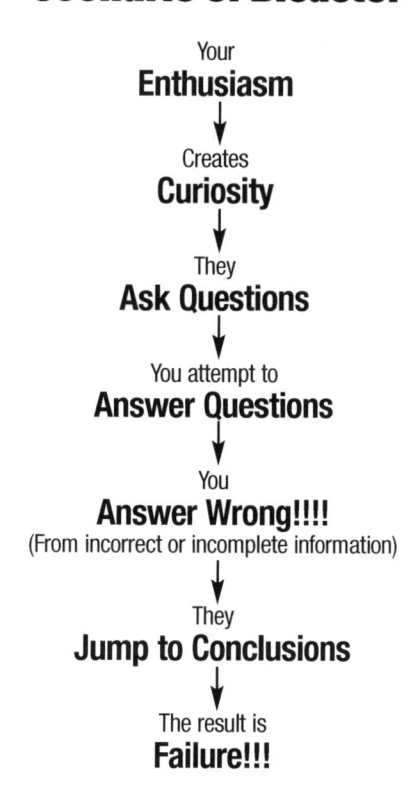

Your
Enthusiasm
↓
Creates
Curiosity
↓
They
Ask Questions
↓
You attempt to
Answer Questions
↓
You
Answer Wrong!!!!
(From incorrect or incomplete information)
↓
They
Jump to Conclusions
↓
The result is
Failure!!!

Points to Remember in Making Contact:

1) **Show enthusiasm.**
   Don't be tentative. We have a first-class, professional, quality company.

2) **Don't get into extensive questions and answers.**
   For you, it's premature. Let them hear it from our experienced leadership.

3) **Bring the person to the meeting yourself.**
   Arrange to pick them up, meet at a neutral site or give clear directions to your office.

4) **Whenever possible, invite both husband and wife.**
   They are both decision makers.

5) **Master the invitation script.**
   This gives you the verbal tools to effectively communicate who we are and what we do. Learn to be a mobile inviter.

STEP 2: The Approach/Contact

Controlling the Point of Contact

Purpose: To effectively contact a prospect and set a date to attend the next Business Opportunity Presentation (BOP) at the office, or alternatively, a one-on-one BOP in the next 24-48 hours.

The New Supercharged Video Drop System/"The Play"

The Key: Run "The Play"

The best way to maximize the HGI opportunity and take advantage of the revolutionary Infinity Compensation & Recognition Plan is to run "The Play."

Every new person must immediately be armed with 10 powerful HGI brochures/video links (hgiplay.com). Each person should experience a minimum 20% success rate and recruit at least two new people. The rapid, relentless repetition of the new Supercharged Video Drop System will ignite the greatest recruiting explosion in the history of world business.

"The Play" will be the catalyst for helping hundreds of thousands of families worldwide realize their dreams and position HGI to Recruit the Planet.

The Video Drop System helps solve many of the problems in contacting prospects:

- You don't go out alone (the company's key Leaders are with you).
- You don't have to make a presentation.
- You don't answer questions, the brochure and video link (hgiplay.com) will do that.

This is the powerful method Hubert Humphrey used to orchestrate his greatest recruiting months ever in his field era. Hubert's massive team recruited nearly 50,000 new associates by dropping almost 150,000 brochures/video links in 90 days.

Why Master the HGI Video Drop?

One associate using the brochure/video links (hgiplay.com) and the LFS:

Cycle	People	10 Brochures	Move Twice	Recruit 20 percent
1	1	10	20	4
2	5	50	100	20
3	25	250	500	100
4	125	1,250	2,500	500
5	625	6,250	12,500	2,500

This example shows closing only External Usage (EU) sales on half of the 80 percent non-recruits who saw the brochure/video:

Cycle	People	10 Brochures	Move Twice	Half of 80 percent
1	1	10	20	8
2	5	50	100	40
3	25	250	500	200
4	125	1,250	2,500	2,000
5	325	6,250	12,500	10,000

This is a hypothetical scenario for illustrative purposes only. There is no assurance that these results can or will be achieved. Cycles represent each distribution of brochures/Videos.

STEP 2 / The Approach/Contact

For educational and training purposes only.

STEP 2: The Approach/Contact

Controlling the Point of Contact

Purpose: To effectively contact a prospect and set a date to attend the next Business Opportunity Presentation (BOP) at the office, or alternatively, a one-on-one BOP in the next 24-48 hours.

The New Supercharged Video Drop System Flow

Pre-Drop Preparation:

- Train your team how to run the Video Drop System.
- Arm your team with 10 HGI brochures and video link flyers (hgiplay.com) each.
- Be prepared to arm every new recruit with 10 HGI brochures, video link flyer (hgiplay.com) and an LFS Manual.
- Have a game plan for distributing the brochures/video link flyer (hgiplay.com).
- Group your prospects geographically to save time.
- Your main goal should be to get 10 brochures with video links out ASAP following the system.
- The best way to execute the actual brochure/video links drop is to do so unannounced. If you feel the need to call them, do so from your cell phone when you are just minutes away from their home.
- Remember the only thing you need to tell people in response to any questions they may ask is, "Just read the brochure and watch the videos." Don't get into any other details with them. Avoid the "Scenario of Disaster" at all costs.
- It is also important to go ahead and schedule the time with your Leader to do the Three-Way Teleconferencing Follow-Up within 24-48 hours after you do the drop.

The Video Drop:

You can't fail. How complicated is it? You drop the brochure/video link invitation (hgiplay.com) off if they're home. If they are not home you drop it off anyway.

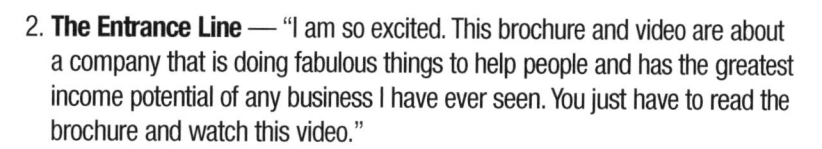

1. **Show Enthusiasm** — Body language is everything.

2. **The Entrance Line** — "I am so excited. This brochure and video are about a company that is doing fabulous things to help people and has the greatest income potential of any business I have ever seen. You just have to read the brochure and watch this video."

3. **Hand them the brochure and flyer containing the video link (hgiplay.com).**

4. **The Exit Line** — "I know you want to know more, but I don't have the time right now. Read the brochure and watch the video and I will get back with you in the next 24-48 hours, unless you get back with me first. Thanks a lot. I will talk with you soon."

You are out of there! Never stay and review the brochure and the video with them.

STEP 2: The Approach/Contact

The 3-Way Teleconference Follow-Up

The Purpose: The objective of this 3-way call is to activate the "Greed" and "Curiosity" buttons of the new prospect to intrigue them to attend the BOP and sign-up with HGI.

The first thing a new recruit has is a believability problem with their friends and associates. The prospect brings the "trust factor" and the upline Leader brings the "believability factor."

The Upline Leader calls the new prospect and says:

"Hello _____ (new prospect), this is _____ (Leader). I'm a _____ (leader's title) with Hegemon Group International and I'm working with _____ (new Associate), who is one of our top up and coming leaders in the area. When I asked _____ (new Associate) who were some of the most ambitious people he/she knew, your name was on the top of the list. I know _____ (new Associate) gave you one of our brochures and videos. Did you get a chance to look at them?"

If they say, "NO, I haven't looked at it yet," the Upline Leader then says:

"No problem, but this company is attracting a lot of attention and the brochures and VIDEOs are in great demand. I need to send _____ (new Associate) by to pick them up by tomorrow. I encourage you to look through the brochure and watch the video before _____ (new Associate) comes by. Then you can decide if this is the right opportunity for you."

If they say, "YES, I've looked at it," without hesitation, the Upline Leader then says:

"Great, _____ (new Associate) and I are really excited about this. HGI is doing fabulous things to help people, and has the greatest income potential of any opportunity I have ever seen. You're not going to believe what a dynamic team _____ (new Associate) is building. At the pace he/she is going, he/she should be earning a second income of more than $100,000 in the next six months. _____ (new Associate) is here with me now and wants to say hello."

Recruit then says:

"_____ new prospect), I have never seen anything like this. The income potential here is truly amazing, and you know if I can do it, you can do it. I'm going to give you back to _____ (leader). What a great leader he/she is. _____ (Leader) is living proof that this business really works.

Upline then says:

"_____ (new prospect), I'm sure you want to learn how to double or triple your income over the next few months. You'll need to rearrange your schedule to give an hour or so to check this out – on either this Tuesday or Thursday night at 7:30. Which of those two nights is best for you?" (wait for answer) "Great _____ (new Associate) will come by your home around _:___ to pick you up or you can just follow him/her to the office. I look forward to seeing you _____ night."

If they say, "YES" with hesitation or if they resist, the Upline Leader then says:

"_____ (new prospect) I know you're busy just like everybody else, but I can tell you are the type of person who wants to make a lot more money while increasing your quality of life. Am I right?"

If they say, "YES" go back to the script.

If they say, "NO," then the Upline Leader says:

"I understand _____ (new prospect). _____ (new Associate) and I have some other calls to make, but we would love to get with you if your circumstances change. Worst case, we need to get with you to show you some of our consumer-oriented concepts and products that could save you and your family thousands of dollars without asking for any new money."

(Go ahead and schedule a time for a financial needs-analysis (FNA) appointment with your field builder.)

The key is to put your upline leader to work helping you follow-up with your Brochure/video drops to maximize your results.

VIDEO MOVEMENT/CIRCULATION REPORT

HGI — HEGEMON GROUP INTERNATIONAL

NAME _____   WEEK OF _____

	No. of brochures purchased this week	No. of brochures/video links placed this week	No. of brochures picked up this week	No. of new associates recruited this week	No. of Product Presentations	No. of sales this week

Prospect Name	Telephone Number	Date Placed	Date of Phone Follow-Up	Date Attended BOP	Date Brochures Picked Up	Match-Up Field Builder	Date Recruited	Data	Business Value on Sale
1									
2									
3									
4									
5									
6									
7									
8									
9									
10									
11									
12									
13									
14									
15									
16									
17									
18									
19									
20									

STEP 3: The Presentation

Business Opportunity Presentation
Purpose: Show the power of the opportunity.

There is no meeting more important than your next Business Opportunity Presentation (BOP).

By running the System and creating an exciting, quality, professional recruiting environment — MoZone — you:

1. Resell the power of the opportunity to existing leaders.
2. Teach existing leaders to sell power of the opportunity.
3. Sell power of the opportunity to new prospects and set a follow-up Get Started Interview in the next one or two days.

Your entire presentation must be compelling and powerful, and conducted by your most enthusiastic and dynamic leaders. But even if you don't have the greatest speakers in the world, don't let that become a negative. Capitalize on the magic of crowds, the synergy that is created by large groups of people — MoZone.

- **The BOP**
  The psychology of the BOP has proven to be highly successful.
  All you have to do is learn how to master it.

- **The One-on-One BOP**
  The second option is the one-on-one BOP. Focus on how to make a powerful, in-home presentation.

POSSIBILITY PROJECTIONS FOR INVITEES

Business Opportunity Presentation Leader: _____   Business Opportunity Presentation Date: _____
Location: _____

#	Name	Invitee's Name	Phone	New or Active	Upline	Committed to Attend
1						
2						
3						
4						
5						
6						
7						
8						
9						
10						
11						
12						
13						
14						
15						
16						
17						
18						
19						
20						
21						
22						
23						
24						
25						

(Includes New Prospects & Existing Team Members Contacted & Committed to Attend)

Office BOP Protocol

PURPOSE:
To create a quality, professional recruiting environment.

MOZONE AT THE OFFICE: (MO-ZONE = MOMENTUM ZONE)

1. Be Prepared Mentally.
Your enthusiasm, conviction, and team spirit will have a tremendous influence on the impression we make.

2. Remember, people respond based on what they feel more than what they hear.
Studies have shown that what is really communicated to people is based on the following:
- 7% content (verbal)
- 38% tone of voice
- 55% body language

We are not just attracting people to a business, we are going to attract them to our **environment**! The atmosphere of the office at the BOP or at any training session is crucial to a successful recruiting meeting. Arrive 1/2 hour before the Business Opportunity Presentation begins so that you and your guests can help create and benefit from the "MOZONE."

3. Professional Appearance.
You must be dressed for a business meeting. Proper business attire (coat and tie for men and appropriate business attire for women) is to be worn by all guests and team members.

4. When you arrive, go directly into the Business Opportunity Meeting Room.
Circulate and help, create a friendly atmosphere. Make sure you personally greet each guest. Stay in the meeting room until after the announcements have been made and you are dismissed for classes, etc...
1) **Do not** hang around in the halls, lobby, sidewalk, parking lot, etc... If you are waiting for a guest, wait in the Business Opportunity Meeting Room only.
2) **Do not** neutralize the excitement of the environment with technical details or negatives.

5. Have ALL guests sign the register, and get a name tag.
(Use standard name badges – red for new guests, blue for existing associates.)

6. Properly use "Leadership Edification."
Introduce your guest(s) to your leaders and the speaker. This helps develop a closeness between the speaker and your guest(s). Make sure to use your guest's name often during conversation with the speaker to insure the name will be remembered through association, and used in interaction during the meeting. Remember, the use of a person's name is a positive form of recognition.

7. Find your guest(s) a seat near the front.
Fill in existing seats before requesting new ones to be set up. There will be a chair monitor; you and your guests don't set up chairs! Do not sit with your guest(s) unless you are staying for the entire meeting.

8. If you're not going to be staying in the meeting with your guest(s)...
Tell them that while they're spending time with _____, you will be in the next room in the training class and that you will meet them as soon as the meeting is over, and to enjoy their time with _____.

9. If you're going to be staying in the meeting with your guest(s)...
1) **Do not** talk during the meeting.
2) **Do not** answer questions the speaker asks the crowd during the meeting.
3) **Do not** get up and leave during the meeting.
4) **Remember,** before and after the meeting is for the **guests**. If you have any questions, comments or things you need to take care of, wait until **all** of the **guests** are gone.

10. Toward the end of the meeting, RMDs and other leaders will be introduced.
People who hold these positions have earned the right to be introduced individually and these leaders typically will be setting the Get Started interview.

WHILE THE MEETING IS IN SESSION:
It is imperative that any conversation or business conducted in the lobby or halls be done very quietly so as not do disturb or distract those in the meeting! Also, never re-enter the meeting once it is in session. Late guests must be handled one-on-one.

STEP 3 / The Presentation

STEP 3: The Presentation

One-on-One/Home BOPs

1. **One-on-One BOPs**

WHAT?	When you can't get the prospect to a big BOP night, take it to them (use the current Leaders With Vision flip chart).
WHERE?	Home, office, restaurant, work, where two or more are gathered.
WHEN?	Breakfast time, mid-morning, lunchtime, afternoons, dinnertime, evenings (anytime and all-the-time).
	4 to 5 days/nights per week.
WHO?	Friends, neighbors, relatives, co-workers, social contacts, business associates (anybody and everybody).
HOW?	With enthusiasm and emotion. Speed width/speed depth. Feed into group BOPs.

2. **Home BOPs**
   - The current HGI BOP presentation
   - Three to 10 key couples
   - BOP Decision Kit/brochure and video.
   - Enthusiasm about opportunity
   - Feed into group BOPs
   - Two to three per week

One-on-One/Home BOP Follow up:

If the person decides they want to join immediately, set a date for them to attend a hiring interview or the next BOP at the office, whichever comes first. If they decide not to join, collect/review their data to determine which of our products are best for them.

Sample script:

"No problem, but as you can tell, our product concepts alone can make a huge impact on your family. We need to at least review your personal information to see which of our concepts is best for you and will save your family the most money. Fair enough?"

STEP 4: The Follow-Up

Mastering the Art of the Follow-Up

Purpose: To move the prospect through filters 1-4 of the Eight Speed Filters.

THE FOLLOW-UP

Just as important as controlling the point of contact on the front-end, the follow-up is equally critical on the back-end. The objective of the follow-up is always to move the prospect through the first four Speed Filters as quickly as possible.

The filters do exactly what they say. They filter out the people who are not serious about the opportunity, and allow you to focus on the ones who are. You can tell a person's commitment level by how far and how fast they move through the Eight Speed Filters.

When the follow-up is properly executed, you will help save people from themselves and you will recruit a higher percentage of people. At the same time, you will have a higher volume of production — a by-product of running the system.

The Follow-Up Process (Speed Filters No. 1 - 4)

1. Stay After the Meeting.
2. Get a Decision Kit.
3. Set a Get Started Interview.
4. Keep the Appointment and Sign Up.

(Filters No. 5 - 8 will be covered in Step 5 – The Start-Up.)

STEP 4 | The Follow-Up

Mastering the Art of the Follow-Up

Purpose: To move the prospect through filters 1-4 of the Eight Speed Filters.

The LFS Eight Speed Filters

The Speed Filters are the best way to keep a new recruit on track for success, and are the ultimate indicators of interest.

Speed Filters 1-4 — Step 4: The Follow-Up
Filter No. 1 – Stay After the Meeting.

If your guest doesn't want to hurry out the door, and wants to stay after the meeting, this is your first sign that you have a potential hot new recruit.

When the meeting ends, go directly to your guest(s), set a positive mood, and say: "Wasn't that great? Here is a copy of our products and services overview, now let's get a decision kit." Don't ask them what they think, or ask them any other questions.

If they agree: Take your guest(s) to get a kit, then meet with your Leader to set up an appointment for a Get Started Interview. If they resist, or don't want to buy a kit, say: "Ok, but I promised _____ that we'd say good night before we left." Stay in control, and turn and walk toward your Leader. When you get there, say, "_____ wanted to say goodbye."

The Leader then says, "It was great having you here. Did you get a kit?" (WFA) When the prospect says "no," the leader then says, "why not?" (in a very polite manner). This question gives the experienced Leader the opportunity to identify and overcome any objections and/or questions that the prospect has that has caused them not to get a kit. Worse case, if the prospect decides they don't want to join, the Leader can then set an appointment to review their data to determine which of our products are best for them.

Filter No. 2 – Get a Decision Kit.

If your new recruit buys a decision kit, you know they are serious about learning more about the opportunity.

The reason we "sell" the kit to the new prospects instead of giving it to them is because everyone will take something if it's free. It would then be impossible to determine their level of seriousness.

The Leader will review the kit and explain why it costs $10. The kit should include the following items in one envelope:

- Promo flyer for link to HGI videos (hgiplay.com)
- "The Play" brochure
- "How To Win The Money Game"
- "Leverage the Winds of Fortune" brochure
- Getting Started Check List and Fast Start Check List

Brochures can be purchased at the HGISuccessStore.com
Printable PDFs are available at HGIUniversity.com

For educational and training purposes only.

STEP 4 / The Follow-Up

STEP 4 — The Follow-Up

Mastering the Art of the Follow-Up

Purpose: To move the prospect through filters 1-4 of the Eight Speed Filters.

Filter No. 3 – Set a Get Started Interview.

Setting a time to attend a Get Started interview is the next filter in determining the commitment level of your new guest.

When setting the appointment, be supportive to the person making the appointment. Let the Leader handle any objections the guest might have.

If your guest(s) need to reschedule his/her appointment, tell them to call the person with whom they set the appointment, and to do so as soon as possible. Once you find out a need for rescheduling, immediately call your Leader and let him know your guest will be calling to reschedule.

Filter No. 4 – Keep the Appointment and Sign Up.

This is the last, and most important, filter in step 4 - The Follow-Up. When a new prospect returns for the Get Started Interview and joins the company, it is the sign of a major commitment from a person who is very serious about the business.

STEP 5 — The Start-Up

The Get Started Interview Outline

The main focus of the Get Started Interview is to get the new person started and get them through Filters 5-8 and get them off to a Fast Start.

- You should have the following tools to conduct all interviews:
    - Get Started Interview Outline
    - Getting Started Check List
    - Fast Start Check List
    - Memory Jogger
    - Top 25 Target Market List Form
    - The Video Movement Report/Circulation Report
    - Infinity Compensation & Recognition Plan Brochure
    - Referral Letter
    - The Business Plan Worksheet
    - Mortgage Pre-App Check List
    - GRA/GRM Referral Sheet

Key Focal Points

- Make sure the Get Started Interview is conducted at the office during the daytime.
- The trainee should be present, if possible, and positively reinforce the Leader.
- Spend the first 5-10 minutes of the interview building a rapport with the new prospect.
- The following questions should serve as an outline for your interview. Ask these questions:

    1) Tell me a little about yourself, where you're from, about your interests, where you went to school, your business background, etc...
    2) From what you have seen and heard so far about Hegemon Group International, what aspects of it intrigue you the most?
    3) If you were going to give this business a try, why would you do it?
    4) Do you have any questions about any particular aspect of our company or business?
    5) From what you've told me, I can't think of one logical reason for you not to give this business a try, can you?
    6) Do you want strong Leadership or weak Leadership from me?
        - A weak Leader doesn't run the system and leaves everything to chance.
        - A strong Leader is someone who will walk you through each step and leaves nothing to chance.

- There are four items we need to get completed right away to get you started:

    1) Complete the HGI sign-up process once this interview is complete:
        - Get the HGI Associate Membership Agreement filled out online.
        - Complete the Getting Started Check List.
        - Complete the Fast Start Check List.
    2) Identify Top 25 Prospect List, and purchase 10 Success From Home Brochures/Conquer Your Future VIDEOs to start the Video Drop System/run "The Play."
    3) Get in the field with your Field Builder within 24-48 hours for a Fast Start.
    4) Set a time to meet with the recruit and his/her spouse to develop their business plan and review their data to see which products meet their needs.

(See LFS Manual, page 60.)

STEP 5: The Start-Up

The Fast Start Challenge

Purpose: Leader gets new Associate off to a Fast Start by quickly completing Speed Filters 5-8.

THE START-UP

Just as the first few days of an infant's life are critical to his/her health and well-being, the first few days for a new recruit set the tone for his/her business career.

While all the components of the start-up are important, nothing is more critical than beginning to build the recruit's business by surrounding him/her with new recruits. You must instill in the new recruit a 100 percent commitment to growth from day one.

- **The Start-Up Process (Speed Filters No. 5 - 8)**
    - Develop a Prospect List.
    - Set Goals/Create Business Plan.
    - Match-Up with Field Builder for Fast Start to Quality Associate.
    - Review Personal Data in the Home.

- **Field Building**

    Field Building is a very important area of focus and activity in your business. To succeed, you must become a field-building expert and establish the prototype for your teammates to duplicate.

- **The Sales Process**

    Remember, every presentation is a recruiting presentation. Always sell HGI's concepts first, and close every presentation by asking for referrals.

STEP 5 — *The Start-Up*

The Fast Start Challenge

Purpose: Leader gets new Associate off to a Fast Start by quickly completing Speed Filters 5-8.

Speed Filters 5-8 — Step 5: The Start-Up

Filter No. 5 – Develop a Prospect List.

When a new recruit is willing to create a prospect list, you know they are excited about our opportunity and they're willing to share it with people they know.

- Start one on the spot and you as the Leader, lead the way. Have the spouse participate when possible.

- Qualify Top 25 for a Fast Start.

- Teach new recruit how to become a master inviter and review the Scenario of Disaster.

- Use the 3-part Top 25 prospect list forms. You keep a copy of the Prospect List to help track and monitor the new recruit's progress. The other copy goes to the upline RMD.

- Also, to maximize the new recruit's influence, make sure to get them to sign 25 referral letters.

(See LFS Manual, page 18.)

Filter No. 6 – Set Goals/Create Business Plan.

When the new recruit shares his dreams with you and sets goals to accomplish them, you know they are starting on the path to success. Review the components of a Winning Business Plan and their Business Plan worksheet to help them get started.

(See LFS Manual, page 64.)

STEP 5 / The Start-Up   For educational and training purposes only.

STEP 5 — The Start-Up

The Fast Start Challenge

Purpose: Leader gets new Associate off to a Fast Start by quickly completing Speed Filters 5-8.

Filter No. 7 – Match-Up with Field Builder for Fast Start to Quality Associate.

One of the strongest indications of a person's commitment is when they take action and begin to build their team.

1. Assign a Field Builder to every new recruit immediately.

2. The Field Builder controls the point of contact as the new recruit uses the video drop system to get new prospects to the next BOP. The new recruit should buy 10 brochures/VIDEOs and circulate them at least two and a half times, which should result in 10-15 presentations.

3. The Field Builder holds one-on-one BOPs with the new recruit (for those who don't attend a group BOP).

4. The Field Builder conducts Get Started interviews.

(See LFS Manual, page 92.)

5. The Field Builder completes the Financial Needs Analysis (FNA) on the new recruit's prospects and helps them make their field training sales. Refer to the Field Building section on page 77 of the LFS Manual for more details.

6. Make sure each new recruit immediately signs up with HGI to ensure that they are quality recruits.

7. Qualify for the Fast Start Award with 5 new quality personal recruits and 5 qualified field training sales in the first 30 days.

Filter No. 8 – Review Personal Data in the Home.

When a new recruit completes their personal data and their Financial Needs Analysis (FNA) you know you have a commited recruit who believes in what we do for people. It's tough to commit others to something that you yourself don't practice.

- Leader reviews the data for new associate and spouse and helps them determine which concepts and products fit their individual needs.

For educational and training purposes only.

STEP 5 / The Start-Up

STEP 5: The Start-Up

The Fast Start Challenge

Purpose: Leader gets new Associate off to a Fast Start by quickly completing Speed Filters 5-8.

The Get Started Interview Outline

The main focus of the Get Started Interview is to get the new person started and get them through Filters 5-8 and get them off to a Fast Start.

- You should have the following tools to conduct all interviews:
  - Get Started Interview Outline
  - Getting Started Check List
  - Fast Start Check List
  - Memory Jogger
  - Top 25 Target Market List Form
  - The Video Movement Report/Circulation Report
  - Infinity Compensation & Recognition Brochure
  - Referral Letter
  - The Business Plan Worksheet
  - HGI Referral Sheet

Key Focal Points

- Make sure the Get Started Interview is conducted at the office during the daytime.
- The trainee should be present, if possible, and positively reinforce the Leader.
- Spend the first 5-10 minutes of the interview building a rapport with the new prospect.
- The following questions should serve as an outline for your interview. Ask these questions:

    1) Tell me about yourself, where you're from, about your interests, where you went to school, your business background, etc...

    2) From what you have seen and heard so far about Hegemon Group International, what aspects of it intrigue you the most?

    3) If you were going to give this business a try, why would you do it?

    4) Do you have any questions about any particular aspect of our company or business?

    5) From what you've told me, I can't think of one logical reason for you not to give this business a try, can you?

    6) Do you want strong Leadership or weak Leadership from me?
    - **A weak Leader doesn't run the system and leaves everything to chance.**
    - **A strong Leader is someone who will walk you through each step and leaves nothing to chance.**

- There are four items we need to get completed right away to get you started:

    1) Complete the HGI sign-up process once this interview is complete:
        - Get the HGI Associate Membership Agreement filled out online.
        - Complete the Getting Started Check List.
        - Complete the Fast Start Check List.

    2) Identify Top 25 Prospect List, and purchase 10 brochures and DVD/video links to start the Video Drop System.

    3) Get in the field with your Field Builder within 24-48 hours for a Fast Start.

    4) Set a time to meet with the recruit and his/her spouse to develop their business plan and review their data to see which products meet their needs.

        Sample script: We need to set a time to sit down with you and your spouse to review your data and determine which of our product concepts best fit your needs. Which is the best time for us to get together, tomorrow night or the night after?

Getting Started Check List

Success demands that you complete this entire Check List to maximize the HGI opportunity.

☐ **Join Hegemon Group International:**
- Use your Sponsor's link to complete the sign-up process at HGICrusade.com. Choose either the Gold or Silver Plan. Receive your HGI Member ID and make a note of it.
- Pay your HGI membership and technology fees.* Non-refundable.
- Receive your HGI Member ID and make note of it.

☐ **Review the Features and Links in Your Back Office:**
- Follow all instructions in the "Getting Started Section" of your HGICrusade.com back office.

☐ **Review Product Provider Resources in your HGICrusade.com Back Office:**
- Review Licensed Products under the Innovation Partners and HFG Sections.
- Review the Non-Licensed Products section.

☐ **Getting Licensed:**
- Review the Licensing Resources in your HGICrusade.com back office.

☐ **Complete the HGI Required Documents:**
- Reference the "Required Documents" link under Resources in the HGICrusade.com back office.
- Follow the instructions listed in this section on how to submit your completed forms.

☐ **Complete Your Fast Start Check List**

Fast Start Check List

Success demands urgent completion of this entire Check List to maximize the HGI opportunity.

- ☐ **Complete Getting Started Check List**
- ☐ **Prospecting - Create A Target Market List**
  — Begin to develop your prospect list with a goal of a minimum of 100 names.
  — Use the Executive Memory Jogger to add as many names as possible to your list.
  — Identify the " Top 10/25" on your list and get 10 videos dropped in the first week.
  (If your car broke down in the middle of the night, who would you call?)

- ☐ **The Approach/Contact**
  — Control the point of contact.
  — Avoid the scenario of disaster.
  Your enthusiasm creates curiosity. They ask questions. You attempt to answer questions.
  You answer wrong!!! (From incorrect or incomplete information.) They jump to conclusions. The result is failure!!!
  — Match-Up with your Field Builder and begin running the Video Drop System/" The Play"

- ☐ **Order Your Marketing Tools**

  — Login to HGICrusade.com and be sure your Gold or Silver package is activated to be eligible to earn commissions and full overrides on all product sales from you and your team.
  — Visit www.HGISuccessStore.com and order all of your supplies:

  - Business Cards
  - Video Drop System Materials:
    - Decision Kit Materials: (5 each of: *How to Win the Money Game*, *The Play*, *Leverage the Winds of Fortune*)
    - 10 Copies of the *Secrets of Money*
  - Reference materials:
    - Leadership Format System Manual
    - Unlocking the Secrets of the System Book (5 copies)
    - Magic of Compound Recruiting Book
  - Recommended items to download and print:
    - 10 copies of the Video Link Invitation
    - 20 copies of HGI Products and Services Brochure
    - HGI All-the-Forms Document (print individual pages as needed)

- ☐ **Plan To Attend Upcoming Company Events**
  — Next Local Meeting: _____ Date: _____
  — Next Company Big Event: _____ Date: _____
  — Other Upcoming Events: _____ Date: _____

- ☐ **The Presentation – BOP & One-on-One**
  — Get your prospects to the next meeting - or take the meeting to them one-on-one.
  — Commit to attend all weekly BOP meetings and company events for ongoing training and motivation.
  — Dress for all BOP meetings is business - coat and tie for men and business attire for women.

- ☐ **Complete Your Personal Data**
  — Review all of our products and services for your personal needs.

- ☐ **Start Training Process With Certified Field Builder**
  — Field Builder assigned by upline RMD.
  — Match-Up with your Field Builder for a Fast Start to Quality Associate.
  — Fast Start Award - 5 personal recruits and 5 qualified Field Training sales in first 30 days.

- ☐ **Set An Appointment With Your Leader Within the First 24-48 Hours**
  — Discuss your product and service needs.
  — Make sure your spouse is recruited and committed to the business.
  — Finish your prospect list and any other paperwork.

For educational and training purposes only.

The 6 Components of a Great Business Plan
"Your Plan to Turn Your Desires into Gold."

(You must complete this worksheet specifically and exactly to make your dreams come true.)

_____ _____
Current Level   Next Promotion Level

_____ _____
Current Production   Promotion Requirements

1) Exact amount of new associates_____, sales_____, points_____, income_____ you desire each month.

2) Exactly what you will give in return for this:

   _____ Number of evenings/hours per week

   _____ Number of video Drops per week

   _____ Number of BOP invitations per week

   _____ Number of BOP attendees per week

   _____ Number of Get Started interviews per week

   _____ Number of new recruits per week

   _____ Number of product presentations per week

   _____ Number of new clients per week

3) Definite date when you will possess the recruits, sales, points and income: _____

4) Definite date when you will write out your clear, concise detailed
   statement and plan: _____

5) Definite date you will turn your plan into action: _____

6) Definite times each day when you will read aloud your written statement,
   while vividly imagining yourself in possession of the income and
   new associates: _____ a.m.

                                                            _____ p.m.

STEP 5 — The Start-Up

The Fast Start Challenge

Purpose: Leader gets new Associate off to a Fast Start by quickly completing Speed Filters 5-8.

Master the Art of Field Building

Three HGI Absolutes

In order to participate in company contests, incentive trips, bonus pools, equity sharing credit pool or any company recognition programs and elite clubs, you must implement:

- Every new associate must immediately sign up with HGI.
- Every new associate must immediately be assigned a Field Builder and complete all field training requirements.
- Every new associate must immediately have at least one new recruit.

The No. 1 responsibility of every leader in HGI – from Associate to CEOMD – is to be a Field Builder.

- The Field Builder is responsible for training the new recruit:
  - Prospecting and Video Drop System – "The Play"
  - A Winning Presentation
  - Get Started Interview
  - Making the Sale

- Field Build the new associate with the goal of having 5-10 new recruits in the first few weeks.
- Input a minimum of 3 qualified field training sales.

Manage activity for you and your Field Builders.

- Set, maintain and follow-up on standards of excellence.
  - Field Build three to four nights per week and Saturdays — 10 presentations a week.

Field Builder Standards of Excellence
Associate Results when teamed with a Field Builder

	Video Drops/Week	Presentations/Week	Recruits/Week	FNAs/Week	Closed Trans./Week	Income (50%)/Week
Poor	0-9	0-4	0	0	0	$0
Fair	10-14	5-7	1-2	1-2	1	$1,000
Good	15-20	8-10	3-4	3-4	2	$2,000
Great	21-29	11-19	4-5	4-5	3-4	$4,000
Excellent	30+	20+	6+	6+	5+	$5,000+

Personal Standards of Excellence (per week): 10 Video Drops
5 Presentations
2 Recruits
2 Transactions

STEP 5: The Start-Up

The Fast Start Challenge
Purpose: Leader gets new Associate off to a Fast Start by quickly completing Speed Filters 5-8.

Field Building
Every RMD must have at least one Certified Field Builder. HGI Success Ratio: 1 CFB for every 15 recruits.

The Four Key Responsibilities of Field Building
1. Prospecting and Video Drop System ("The Play")
2. A Winning Presentation (Leaders With Vision Flipchart)
3. Get Started Interview
4. Making the Sale – Input Loans/Real Estate Referrals/Sides

How the RMD Builds Field Builders
1. They learn by observing first-hand what you do.
2. Drill For Skill - role play each step with them.
3. Make sure they master each step. (Inspect and certify their ability to complete each step.)
4. RMD delegates responsibility one step at a time.
5. Monitor results to know their effectiveness.

Accountability of Field Builders
Field Builders must update and submit weekly to RMD:
1. Eight Speed Filter Check List
2. Field Builder Match-Up Report
3. Video Movement/Circulation Report for upcoming week for each trainee on Field Builder Match-Up Report
4. Team Leadership Check List

The Definition of a HGI Field Builder:
1. Field Recruiting – the continuous opening of outlets.
2. Field Training – the movement of volume production through the outlets.

Certified Field Builder Requirements:
1. You must be a Quality Associate:
   – Signed up with HGI and associates.
   – Complete field training requirements.
   – Have at least one recruit who has signed up with all companies.
2. You must master these skills and be certified by your RMD:
   – Prospecting and the Video Drop System – "The Play."
   – A Winning Presentation – Leaders With Vision BOP flipchart.
   – The Get Started Interview.
   – Making the Sale – Input Apps
3. You must be in total alignment with HGI and use all of our communication tools:
   – HGI-Online and Company Email
   – The Leader Network

The RMD must take full responsibility that each Certified Field Builder has met all requirements.

STEP 5 — The Start-Up

The Fast Start Challenge

Purpose: Leader gets new Associate off to a Fast Start by quickly completing Speed Filters 5-8.

Field Builder Training and Accountability

Each RMD must meet with their Field Builders on a weekly basis to monitor the progress of all new recruits in the RMD Base. The following is the suggested outline to be used for the meeting agenda.

1. Review Eight Speed Filter Reports

- Review the Speed Filter progress of each new recruit.
- Discuss and schedule follow-up to make sure each new recruit completes their next step.
  (New prospects should remain on the Eight Speed Filter Report no more than seven days.)

2. Review Field Building Match-Up Reports

- Make sure every new recruit is on the report.
- Check last week's activity for each recruit.
- Check last week's Field Building personal activity.
- Check number of videos to be dropped this week.

3. Review Video Circulaton Report

- Each recruit on Field Building Match-Up Report should have at least ten names on this report.
- Review and discuss last week's numbers.

4. Review Leadership Check List.

- Discuss and assign follow-up to make sure new recruit meets all requirements on the Check List.

5. Assign responsibilities for the next BOP, using the BOP Leadership Assignments Form.

6. Drill for Skill.

- Week No. 1 – Prospecting/Video Drop - "The Play"
- Week No. 2 – The Presentation/The BOP
- Week No. 3 – The Start-Up/Getting Started Interview
- Week No. 4 – Making the Sale/Mastering the Art of Field Building
- Week No. 5 – Forward - Start the Cycle Again

For educational and training purposes only.

The Eight Speed Filter Check List

	Name	Phone Number	Inviter's Name	FILTER 1 Stay After BOP/Mozone	FILTER 2 Get the Kit	FILTER 3 Commit to Get Started Interview	FILTER 4 Complete Interview/Sign Up	FILTER 5 Develop Prospect List	FILTER 6 Set Goals/ Business Plan	FILTER 7 FNA/ Internal Consumption	FILTER 8 Match-Up Field Building
1											
2											
3											
4											
5											
6											
7											
8											
9											
10											
11											
12											
13											
14											
15											
16											
17											
18											
19											
20											
21											
22											
23											
24											
25											

HGI
HEGEMON GROUP INTERNATIONAL

(New prospects should remain on the Eight Speed Filter Check List no more than seven days.)

FIELD BUILDER MATCH-UP REPORT

Field Builder _____
RMD _____
Week Of: _____

	NEXT WEEK'S VIDEO DROPS	VIDEO DROPS WEEK	VIDEO DROPS MTD	CONTACTS WEEK	CONTACTS MTD	PRESENTATIONS WEEK	PRESENTATIONS MTD	RECRUITS WEEK	RECRUITS MTD	FNAs WEEK	FNAs MTD	REFERRALS WEEK	REFERRALS MTD	OTHER WEEK	OTHER MTD
Field Builder Personal Activity ------>															
Trainee Name															
1															
2															
3															
4															
5															
6															
7															
8															
9															
10															
11															
12															
13															
14															
TOTALS															

Field Builder updates and turns into RMD weekly.
1. Eight Speed Filter Check List
2. Field Builder Match-Up Report
3. Video Circulation Report for each new recruit
4. Team Leadership Check List

The Field Builder is responsible for driving activity.

Team Leadership Check List

RMD _____

Promotions/Awards	Promoted to RMD
	Promoted to SA
	Promoted to FA
	Fast Start Award
Marketing Tools/Events	Product Provider Links
	HGI University Active
	LFSMAX Gold Active
	Register for Next Event
Own Products	Non-Licensed Provider
	Insurance/Annuity
Field Building Certified	Making the Sale
	Get Started Interview
	A Winning Presentation
	Prospecting/Video Drop System
Match-Up	Match-Up Sales
	Field Builder
Non-Licensed Providers	IC/Customer Sales
	Product Provider Training
HFG	Getting Licensed?
	IC Sale
	FNA
	Contracted/Appointed
	My License Profile
HGI	3 Field Training Sales
	Demonstrated ability to login to all HGI websites
	At least 100 leads loaded into LFSMAX Gold System
	At least 100 leads on list
	W-9 Submitted
	Ordered HGI Business Cards
	Ordered Brochures for "The Play and Decision Kits"
	Complete 8 Speed Filters

Recruit Name

Field Builder updates and turns into RMD weekly
1. Eight Speed Filter Check List
2. Field Builder Match-Up Report
3. Video Circulation Report for each new recruit
4. Team Leadership Check List

STEP 5 : The Start-Up

The Fast Start Challenge

Purpose: Leader gets new Associate off to a Fast Start by quickly completing Speed Filters 5-8.

HGI Speed Calendar

Collapse Time Frames/Compress Activity

"For a thousand years in thy sight are but as yesterday."
— Psalms 90:4

What a powerful paradigm — a thousand years on earth is but a day in the sight of the Lord.

While we'll never be able to collapse time like this, we can become Possibility Thinkers and Impossibility Achievers by compressing a decade into one year ... one year into three months ... three months into one week ... one week into one day ... and one day into three mini-days.

	MONDAY	TUESDAY	WEDNESDAY	THURSDAY	FRIDAY	SATURDAY
7 a.m. TO noon	MINI-DAY 1 Minimum 5 Direct Contacts	MINI-DAY 4 Minimum 5 Direct Contacts	MINI-DAY 7 Minimum 5 Direct Contacts	MINI-DAY 10 Minimum 5 Direct Contacts	MINI-DAY 13 Minimum 5 Direct Contacts	MINI-DAY 16 Minimum 5 Direct Contacts
12:01 to 6 p.m.	MINI-DAY 2 Minimum 5 Direct Contacts	MINI-DAY 5 Minimum 5 Direct Contacts	MINI-DAY 8 Minimum 5 Direct Contacts	MINI-DAY 11 Minimum 5 Direct Contacts	MINI-DAY 14 Minimum 5 Direct Contacts	MINI-DAY 17 Minimum 5 Direct Contacts
6:01 p.m. to midnight	MINI-DAY 3 PRIME TIME 7-10 p.m. Minimum 5 Direct Contacts	MINI-DAY 6 PRIME TIME 7-10 p.m. Minimum 5 Direct Contacts	MINI-DAY 9 PRIME TIME 7-10 p.m. Minimum 5 Direct Contacts	MINI-DAY 12 PRIME TIME 7-10 p.m. Minimum 5 Direct Contacts	MINI-DAY 15 PRIME TIME 7-10 p.m. Minimum 5 Direct Contacts	MINI-DAY 18 PRIME TIME 7-10 p.m. Minimum 5 Direct Contacts

Total Combustion Super Blitz Campaign

"I expect every HGI RMD/Leader to MAX-OUT all 6 days (18 Mini-Days) each week for one full 90-Day Madman Cycle." — Hubert Humphrey

If you are not yet full-time with HGI, simply fill in the time slots which you have to devote to building your HGI business.

HGI Speed Calendar

_____ (Month)

Monday	Tuesday	Wednesday	Thursday	Friday	Saturday
Mini-Day 1 7:00 _____ 8:00 _____ 9:00 _____ 10:00 _____ 11:00 _____	Mini-Day 4 7:00 _____ 8:00 _____ 9:00 _____ 10:00 _____ 11:00 _____	Mini-Day 7 7:00 _____ 8:00 _____ 9:00 _____ 10:00 _____ 11:00 _____	Mini-Day 10 7:00 _____ 8:00 _____ 9:00 _____ 10:00 _____ 11:00 _____	Mini-Day 13 7:00 _____ 8:00 _____ 9:00 _____ 10:00 _____ 11:00 _____	Mini-Day 16 7:00 _____ 8:00 _____ 9:00 _____ 10:00 _____ 11:00 _____
Mini-Day 2 12:00 _____ 1:00 _____ 2:00 _____ 3:00 _____ 4:00 _____ 5:00 _____	Mini-Day 5 12:00 _____ 1:00 _____ 2:00 _____ 3:00 _____ 4:00 _____ 5:00 _____	Mini-Day 8 12:00 _____ 1:00 _____ 2:00 _____ 3:00 _____ 4:00 _____ 5:00 _____	Mini-Day 11 12:00 _____ 1:00 _____ 2:00 _____ 3:00 _____ 4:00 _____ 5:00 _____	Mini-Day 14 12:00 _____ 1:00 _____ 2:00 _____ 3:00 _____ 4:00 _____ 5:00 _____	Mini-Day 17 12:00 _____ 1:00 _____ 2:00 _____ 3:00 _____ 4:00 _____ 5:00 _____
Mini-Day 3 — Prime Time 7:00 p.m.–10:00 p.m. 6:00 _____ 7:00 _____ 8:00 _____ 9:00 _____ 10:00 _____ 11:00 _____ 12:00 _____	Mini-Day 6 — Prime Time 7:00 p.m.–10:00 p.m. 6:00 _____ 7:00 _____ 8:00 _____ 9:00 _____ 10:00 _____ 11:00 _____ 12:00 _____	Mini-Day 9 — Prime Time 7:00 p.m.–10:00 p.m. 6:00 _____ 7:00 _____ 8:00 _____ 9:00 _____ 10:00 _____ 11:00 _____ 12:00 _____	Mini-Day 12 — Prime Time 7:00 p.m.–10:00 p.m. 6:00 _____ 7:00 _____ 8:00 _____ 9:00 _____ 10:00 _____ 11:00 _____ 12:00 _____	Mini-Day 15 — Prime Time 7:00 p.m.–10:00 p.m. 6:00 _____ 7:00 _____ 8:00 _____ 9:00 _____ 10:00 _____ 11:00 _____ 12:00 _____	Mini-Day 18 — Prime Time 7:00 p.m.–10:00 p.m. 6:00 _____ 7:00 _____ 8:00 _____ 9:00 _____ 10:00 _____ 11:00 _____ 12:00 _____

7:00 a.m. to 12:00 Noon
Minimum 5 Direct Contacts per Mini Day

12:01 p.m. to 6:00 p.m.
Minimum 5 Direct Contacts per Mini Day

6:01 p.m. to 12:00 Midnight
Minimum 5 Direct Contacts per Mini Day

HGI™
HEGEMON GROUP INTERNATIONAL

STEP 6: Duplication

The Rapid Repetition of the System

Purpose: To build a business using a system whereby recruiting never stops.

Run a System Whereby Recruiting Never Stops

To become a legend of the future, you must study the legends of the past. The speed and exactness with which you copy the system will in large part determine your success. This cookie-cutter exactness must be duplicated throughout your team.

Remember two things:
1. The key is to imitate, not create.
2. Marketing is the creation of the outlet and the movement of the product simultaneously.

The Hold-A-Meeting System
- The One-On-One BOP
- A Dynamic BOP

Average number of people per week at BOP = Average number of Base Shop sales per month.

Use a BOP Projection Sheet. If you don't prepare to have a good meeting — you won't.

Capture The Magic of Crowds
Monitor the Numbers
Build to Max-out Profits
1. "Wide"
2. "Deep"
3. "Wide" and "Deep"

Three Laws of Building:
1. A recruit is not a recruit until he/she has a recruit.
2. A recruit is not a leg until it is four deep.
3. A leg is not a team until it produces two levels of leaders.

Building Outlets
1. Opening outlets is an all-the-time thing.
2. Have quantity to get quality.

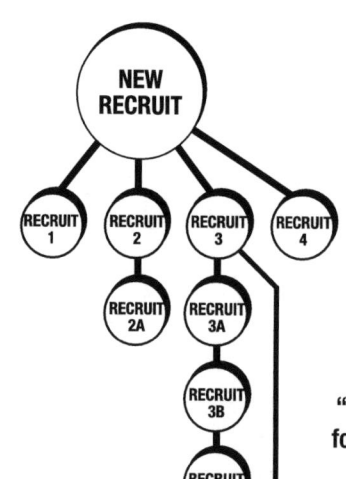

Width = Profitability
Depth = Security

Primary: GO WIDE
Secondary: GO DEEP

"Always focus on going wide. Depth will follow. Remember; you can't have grandchildren until you have children."

Open Outlets and Move Products Simultaneously
- Only 25% of the prospects on a target list will ever come to a BOP.
- If only 100 come to a BOP, you can be assured there are 500 to 600 more who should have come.
- Make sure to offer the opportunity to have a Financial Needs Analysis done for these people.

STEP 6: Duplication

The Rapid Repetition of the System

Purpose: To build a business using a system whereby recruiting never stops.

A Recruiter's Mentality

1. Recruiting is a state of mind.
2. Recruiting is an all-the-time thing.
3. Recruit select masses of people.
4. Recruit quantity to get quality.
5. Every prospect is a recruit until proven differently.
6. Aim at recruits/Hit sales.
7. Recruit and train.
8. Recruit and build.
9. Recruit and motivate.
10. Recruit to win.

"Recruit & Motivate" — The System to Simplify and Multiply

Recruit

Run a system whereby recruiting never stops:

1. Personal speed width = You must commit to and execute four consecutive 90-Day Madman Cycles of personal recruiting/front-line expansion.
2. You've got to constantly have geometric recruiting through your ambitious leaders and constantly identify, at all levels, your recruiting capacitors who can take a big-time recruiting charge from you.
3. The key to exploding big is to build and maintain a minimum 50,000 Business Value AV pure RMD base each month. This is the ONLY WAY you can consistently produce new 1st Generation RMDs.

Motivate

Run a system whereby motivation never stops:

1. Stretch their vision, then motivate them.
2. There's a big difference between a motivated person and a great motivator.
3. To be a great Director of Motivation, you have to constantly, strategically direct your people to proper environment, atmosphere, places, leaders and events that will stretch their vision for you.
4. You can't stretch your own vision, you must submit yourself to great leaders and great visionaries to stretch it for you.

A Builder's Mindset

To Become a HGI Champion You Must Build:

1. A large network of outlets
2. A large base of diversified product-using clients

Two Main Focal Points to Win the Race for Outlets:

1. Get more and more personal direct legs
2. Get more and more people ("old" and "new") to BOPs

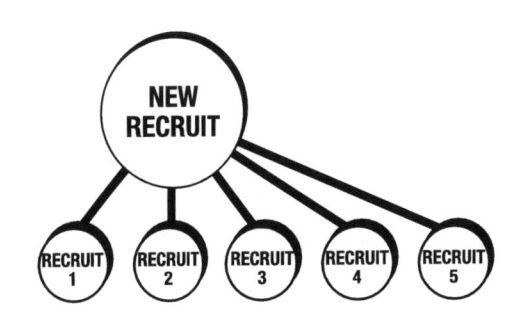

STEP 6: Duplication

The Rapid Repetition of the System

Purpose: To build a business using a system whereby recruiting never stops.

Hubert's Keys to World Domination

The Master Copy Worth Duplicating

1. Hubert Built and Sustained a Great Base Shop RMD Factory.

2. Hubert Built an Ever-Expanding Frontline of Strong 1st Generation RMDs.

3. Hubert Produced 8 to 10 Direct Giant Senior Executive Field Chairman Teams.

4. Hubert Has Always Been a Master Motivator – Super Teams Run on High Octane Motivation.

5. Hubert Has Always Mastered Constant Personal Communication.
    - Motivation
    - Encouragement
    - Good News
    - Know-how
    - Constant Course Correction

6. Hubert Couldn't Live with being Average and Ordinary. He Didn't Just Want to be No. 1. He Needed to be No. 1.

7. Hubert Mastered a System for National Expansion.

    Three Ways Hubert Expanded his Business:
    - He Transplanted Himself to a New Area
    - He Raised Leaders in his Base Shop and Satellited Them Out.
    - He Found Strong Leaders in Certain Areas and Built through Them.

8. Hubert Set Goals of Great Growth of Himself and His Leaders – He Constantly Set Possibility Projections for His Leaders.

To the Leaders Who Build a Big RMD Base Shop and Keep Producing First Generation RMDs Go the Greatest Honors and Greatest Rewards.

STEP 6: Duplication

The Rapid Repetition of the System

Purpose: To build a business using a system whereby recruiting never stops.

LEADERSHIP FORMAT SYSTEM RECRUITING & BUILDING FACTORY

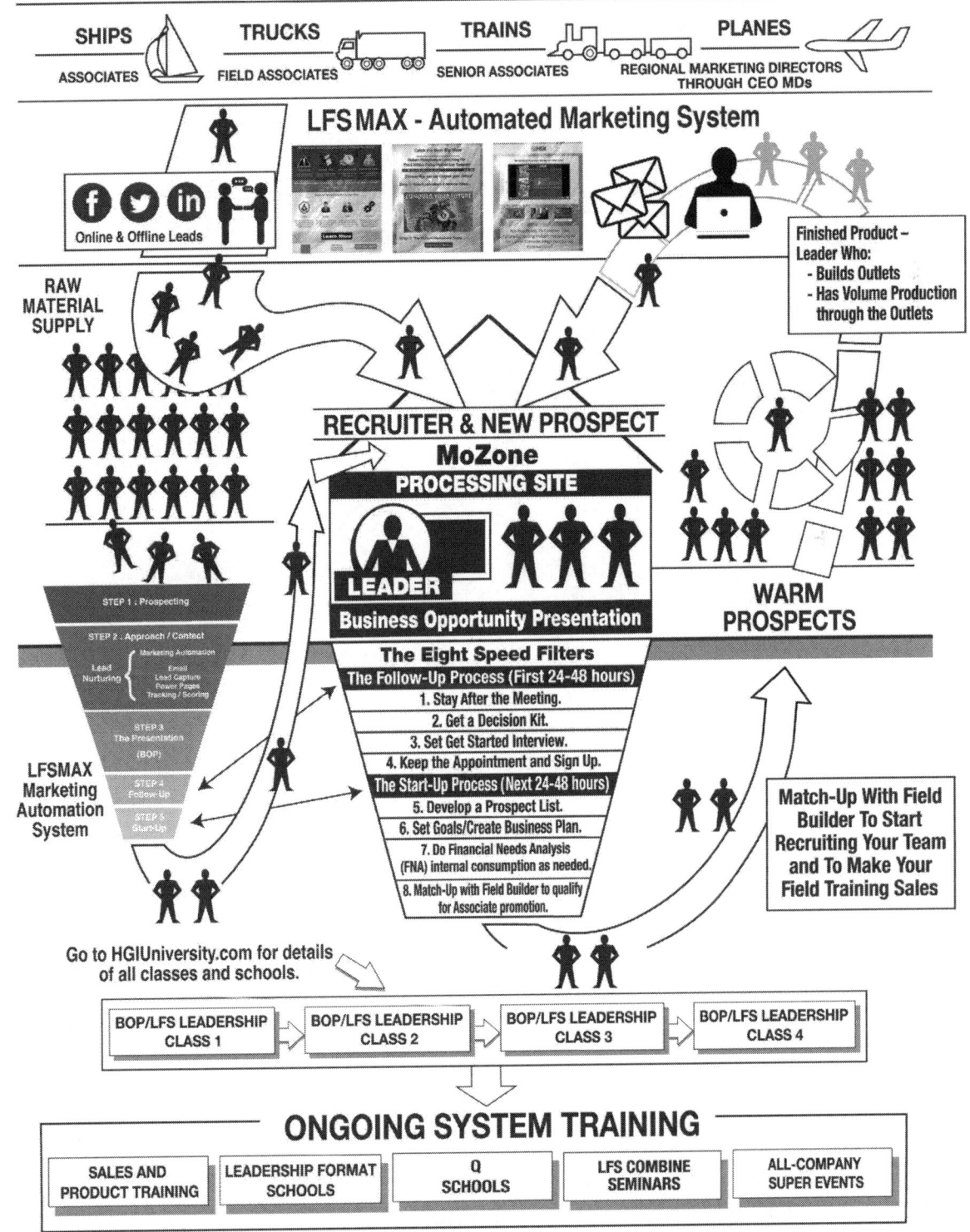

DELIVERY SYSTEM TRANSPORTATION

- **SHIPS** — ASSOCIATES
- **TRUCKS** — FIELD ASSOCIATES
- **TRAINS** — SENIOR ASSOCIATES
- **PLANES** — REGIONAL MARKETING DIRECTORS THROUGH CEO MDs

LFSMAX - Automated Marketing System

Online & Offline Leads

RAW MATERIAL SUPPLY

Finished Product – Leader Who:
- Builds Outlets
- Has Volume Production through the Outlets

RECRUITER & NEW PROSPECT

MoZone PROCESSING SITE

LEADER — Business Opportunity Presentation

WARM PROSPECTS

LFSMAX Marketing Automation System

- STEP 1: Prospecting
- STEP 2: Approach / Contact
  - Lead Nurturing: Marketing Automation, Email, Lead Capture, Power Pages, Tracking / Scoring
- STEP 3: The Presentation (BOP)
- STEP 4: Follow-Up
- STEP 5: Start-Up

The Eight Speed Filters

The Follow-Up Process (First 24-48 hours)
1. Stay After the Meeting.
2. Get a Decision Kit.
3. Set Get Started Interview.
4. Keep the Appointment and Sign Up.

The Start-Up Process (Next 24-48 hours)
5. Develop a Prospect List.
6. Set Goals/Create Business Plan.
7. Do Financial Needs Analysis (FNA) internal consumption as needed.
8. Match-Up with Field Builder to qualify for Associate promotion.

Match-Up With Field Builder To Start Recruiting Your Team and To Make Your Field Training Sales

Go to HGIUniversity.com for details of all classes and schools.

BOP/LFS LEADERSHIP CLASS 1 → BOP/LFS LEADERSHIP CLASS 2 → BOP/LFS LEADERSHIP CLASS 3 → BOP/LFS LEADERSHIP CLASS 4

ONGOING SYSTEM TRAINING

| SALES AND PRODUCT TRAINING | LEADERSHIP FORMAT SCHOOLS | Q SCHOOLS | LFS COMBINE SEMINARS | ALL-COMPANY SUPER EVENTS |

For educational and training purposes only.

STEP 6: Duplication

The Rapid Repetition of the System

Purpose: To build a business using a system whereby recruiting never stops.

The Magic of 90-Day Madman Cycles

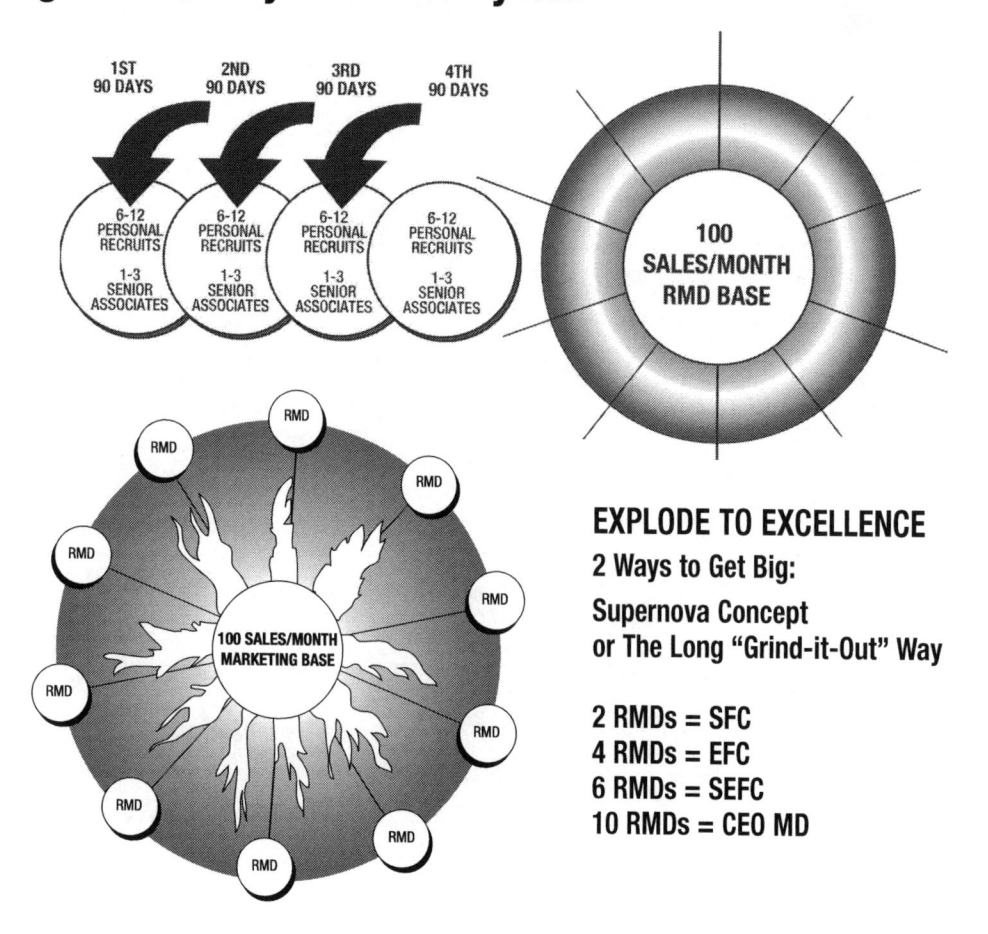

1ST 90 DAYS → 6-12 Personal Recruits / 1-3 Senior Associates
2ND 90 DAYS → 6-12 Personal Recruits / 1-3 Senior Associates
3RD 90 DAYS → 6-12 Personal Recruits / 1-3 Senior Associates
4TH 90 DAYS → 6-12 Personal Recruits / 1-3 Senior Associates

100 SALES/MONTH RMD BASE

100 SALES/MONTH MARKETING BASE (surrounded by RMDs)

EXPLODE TO EXCELLENCE

2 Ways to Get Big:

Supernova Concept
or The Long "Grind-it-Out" Way

2 RMDs = SFC
4 RMDs = EFC
6 RMDs = SEFC
10 RMDs = CEO MD

Top Priority

No. 1. The "continuous opening of outlets"

No. 2. Volume production per outlet

In this business, every person is an outlet. YOU are an outlet. An outlet is anyone who can offer the product to the consumer. The difference between this business and other marketing systems is that as an independent contractor, YOU have the ability to set up your own distribution system within the big network.

The Magic of Duplication

Hubert Humphrey has followed the same system for years. This is the same system that most of his successful Leaders adopted. All recruits joining HGI should follow the same blueprint to duplicate their great success.

The best way to get a high level of performance is to be sure that the master copy is worth duplicating.

STEP 6 / Duplication

For educational and training purposes only.

STEP 6 — Duplication

The Rapid Repetition of the System

Purpose: To build a business using a system whereby recruiting never stops.

The Magic of Compound Recruiting

The Magic Of Multiples

	Each Recruit 2	Difference of ONE	Each Recruit 3
	2		3
Level 1	x2		x3
	4		9
Level 2	x2		x3
	8		27
Level 3	x2		x3
	16		81
Level 4	x2		x3
	32		243
Level 5	x2		x3
	64		729
Level 6	x2		x3
	128		2,187
Level 7	x2		x3
	256		6,561
Level 8	x2		x3
	512		19,683
Level 9	x2		x3
	1,024	Difference of 58,025	59,049

The Magic Of Geometric Progression

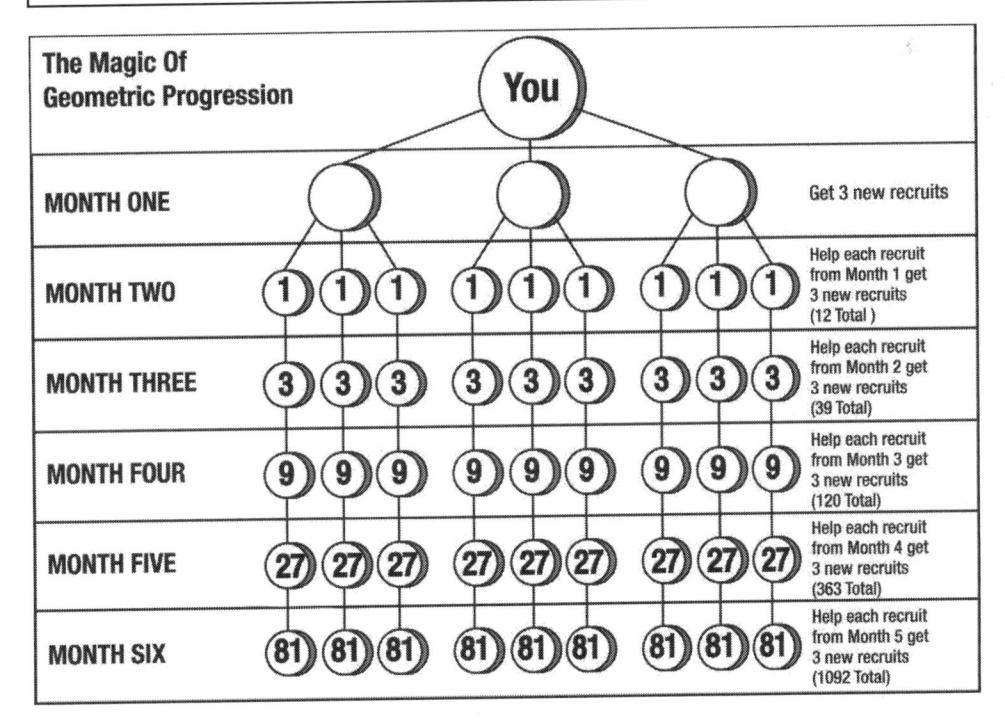

You

- **MONTH ONE** — Get 3 new recruits
- **MONTH TWO** — (1)(1)(1) (1)(1)(1) (1)(1)(1) — Help each recruit from Month 1 get 3 new recruits (12 Total)
- **MONTH THREE** — (3)(3)(3) (3)(3)(3) (3)(3)(3) — Help each recruit from Month 2 get 3 new recruits (39 Total)
- **MONTH FOUR** — (9)(9)(9) (9)(9)(9) (9)(9)(9) — Help each recruit from Month 3 get 3 new recruits (120 Total)
- **MONTH FIVE** — (27)(27)(27) (27)(27)(27) (27)(27)(27) — Help each recruit from Month 4 get 3 new recruits (363 Total)
- **MONTH SIX** — (81)(81)(81) (81)(81)(81) (81)(81)(81) — Help each recruit from Month 5 get 3 new recruits (1092 Total)

This is a hypothetical scenario for illustrative purposes only. There is no assurance that these results can or will be achieved.

For educational and training purposes only.

STEP 6 Duplication

The Rapid Repetition of the System
Purpose: To build a business using a system whereby recruiting never stops.

Conquer Your Future

HGI is looking for the next generation of Modern-Day Alexanders. Like Alexander the Great, whose chief aim was to "Conquer the World and Make it Greek," HGI's Modern-Day Alexanders want to "Conquer the World and Make it Wealthy." Just like Alexander, Hubert Humphrey is looking to build a company-wide group of leaders who are 100% committed to becoming Modern-Day Alexanders to conquer the business world.

Profile of a Member of the Companion Cavalry

- Leaders who are ready to take a big-time recruiting and building charge

- Leaders who are prepared to become bigger stars as a result of being part of the Companion Cavalry

- Leaders who want to build a legacy, like Alexander, to be known as simply "the greatest"

- Leaders who believe in a more noble cause

- Leaders who believe they can change the world

- Leaders who are ready to take the next step... the evolution to Modern-Day Alexanders

This is the official logo of the Companion Cavalry. The Super Team name of your upline EFC or Diamond Club member willl be added below the logo.

Two Main Components of the Army of Conquest Master Plan

Build an "Army of Conquest" committed to becoming the next generation of Modern-Day Alexanders.

Main Component No. 1.
    HGI Plan to Focus
    - Focal Point No. 1: Recruiting

Main Component No. 2.
    Wealth Builder Pathway to CEO MD
    – Focal Point No. 2: Building

For educational and training purposes only.

STEP 6 — Duplication

The Rapid Repetition of the System
Purpose: To build a business using a system whereby recruiting never stops.

Main Component No. 1
HGI Plan To Focus - Focal Point No. 1: Recruiting

You must qualify to wear the Warrior shirts. Any leader, regardless of promotion level, who meets the guidelines qualifies. It's never too early to be building your base.

	10 Base Recruits	On track for CEO MD Team "Companion Cavalry"- white Warrior shirt (with Companion Cavalry logo)/Attend their meetings.
	25 Base Recruits	Inducted into your CEO MD Team "Companion Cavalry"- light blue Warrior shirt (with Companion Cavalry logo)
	50 Base Recruits	On track for Hubert's All-Company "Companion Cavalry" - dark blue Warrior shirt (with Companion Cavalry logo)
	75 Base Recruits	Inducted into the "Royal Elite Guard" of Hubert's All-Company "Companion Cavalry"- light green Warrior shirt (with Companion Cavalry logo)
	100 RMD Base Recruits	Become Hubert's All-Company "Modern-Day Alexander"- gold Warrior shirt (with Modern-Day Alexander logo) *Hubert's main Inner Circle of Warriors who will participate in elite Warrior Summits*

Warrior Circle
- Qualify to attend elite Warrior Summits.

	100 Super Base-1st Recruits/Mo.	Inducted into Hubert's All-Company "Warrior Circle" - khaki Warrior shirt (with Warrior Circle logo)
	200 Super Base-1st Recruits/Mo.	Inducted into Hubert's All-Company "Warrior Circle" - red Warrior shirt (with Warrior Circle logo)
	300 Super Base-1st Recruits/Mo.	Inducted into Hubert's All-Company "Warrior Circle" - black Warrior shirt (with Warrior Circle logo)

For educational and training purposes only.

STEP 6 / Duplication

STEP 6 — Duplication

The Rapid Repetition of the System

Purpose: To build a business using a system whereby recruiting never stops.

Main Component No. 2
Wealth Builder Pathway To CEO MD – Focal Point No. 2: Building

Converting High-Volume Recruiting Into Great Teams

In the Leadership Format System manual, it teaches you about the laws of duplication.

- **Law No. 1** — A recruit is not a recruit until he/she has a recruit.
- **Law No. 2** — A recruit does not become a leg with a life of its own until it is driven at least four deep.
- **Law No. 3** — A leg does not become a team until at least two system leaders have been built in that leg.

This Wealth Builder Pathway to CEO MD is an instant accountability system. People automatically count their recruiting numbers and direct legs to qualify for shirts and pins.

The pin mark of excellence!
Build wide, deep and geometric for long-term wealth and security.

Base Shop Pins

1WD	3WD	6WD	9WD	12WD
1WD = 1 Leg 4 Deep & 5,000 BV/Mo. RMD Base	3WD = 3 Legs 4 Deep each & 25,000 BV/Mo. RMD Base	6WD = 6 Legs 4 Deep each & 50,000 BV/Mo. RMD Base	9WD = 9 Legs 4 Deep & 75,000 BV/Mo. RMD Base	12WD = 12 Legs 4 Deep each & 100,000 BV/Mo. RMD Base

Super Base Warrior Circle Pins

12WD	20WD	30WD
12WD = 12 Legs 4 Deep each & 250,000 BV/Mo. Super Base-1st	90WD = 90 Legs 4 Deep each & 500,000 BV/Mo. Super Base-1st	30WD = 30 Legs 4 Deep & 1,000,000 BV/Mo. Super Base-1st

Made in the USA
Columbia, SC
19 March 2020